CW01662566

ANTI-HERO
MANAGEMENT

# THE INTERGALACTIC JOURNEY OF A MANAGER

## AN ANTI-HERO MINDSET FOR MODERN MANAGEMENT

Renaud Vandewalle

**Renaud Vandewalle/Athriome Publishing Athriome SAS**
**117, rue de charenton**
**75012 Paris, France**
**https://antiheromanagement.com**

Publisher's Note: This is a work of fiction. Names, characters, places, and incidents are a product of the author's imagination. Locales and public names are sometimes used for atmospheric purposes. Any resemblance to actual people, living or dead, or to businesses, companies, events, institutions, or locales is completely coincidental.



**The intergalactic journey of a manager/ Renaud Vandewalle**. --
1st ed.
ISBN 978-2-9595435-0-0

ANTI-HERO
MANAGEMENT

A message for managers:
I dare you to explore
your own management style!

# Foreword

Welcome to a new era of management, shifting from shareholder focus to valuing meaningful work. Together, let's redefine success in leadership and drive significant organisational transformation.

This book is not exclusively for managers or professionals in management. It provides value to any profession involving interactions, regardless of the sector.

For each chapter which introduces concepts, you will find impactful questions which I advise you to answer only if this concept resonates with you. To go even further, you will also find advice or experimentation to help you in getting ideas to start or continue your own exploration.

My international career as a manager at all levels, my love of books and my recent experience in writing a drama conference inspired me to write this volume.

The intention is to share a mindset that brings serenity and extraordinary results to the workplace. I sincerely hope to inspire others.

# CONTENTS

1

# A MANAGER CALLED PATRICK

In the Milky Way galaxy, there is a blue planet named Earth. Its inhabitants have recently gained technologies which affect their lifestyle significantly. It has caused issues like poor health, environmental and geopolitical crises. People are on a quest for meaning. These changes have had a negative impact on the workplace, leading to higher turnover and a disengaged workforce.

On this planet is a man called Patrick, a successful manager. Despite his young age, he has held his role for quite some time. His department's results were not outstanding for the first time in his career, partly because he remained far too long on Planet Micro-

Management - a world in a parallel universe known as 'Management'.

Patrick always took control of others' work or instructed them on the step-by-step process. He was meticulous, or may I say fussy. Although, he held a respectful relationship with his colleagues, he perceived them as unsuccessful. They were not autonomous nor engaged. His private thought even labelled them as misfits. It sounds harsh, but this is what he considered being the harsh truth.

Patrick looked for help. First, he asked his director, with no luck. He found he lacked guidance from his executive team. He was wondering if he was doing something wrong or whether he was going in the right direction. So, he then tried some leadership training courses suggested by the Human Resource department. Those programs promised life changing outcomes within a few weeks, like a magic potion. "Only 5 steps to become a great manager." With a well-known leader saying: "Do what I did and get incredible results." But Patrick was not in the same context, nor had the same experience, skill set, beliefs and values. It did not work for him. The few lessons he learned were short-lived.

One day, his boss came to his office unannounced. He told him his unit (including Patrick) would be laid off if the circumstances did not improve rapidly and significantly. For someone like Patrick, this was a massive blow. He found himself in a state of total confusion. "What did I do wrong?" he asked himself. He thought he had tried everything and explored all the planets in the galaxy of "The Levers of Engagement" from the 'Management' universe. The typical levers were giving promotions, pay raises, and improving flexibility over when and where to work. Nothing appeared to be effective, not even the new professional football table in the wellness room, nor the nights out with the team, such as karaoke or escape games. He did not know what to do next. Eventually, he talked about it with his former mentors. That was not a simple task for him. Feelings of helplessness, shame, and lack of success overwhelmed him. But he concluded he had no choice. Either get help or get sacked; something had to change.

He contacted his old bosses and colleagues he felt close to. A lot of them provided him with many tips, but nothing convincing or that he hadn't already tried. Maybe he did not try enough; who knows?

Graham, one of his early employers, told him: "Go and hire an Anti-Hero Coach".

"What? Anti-Hero Coach?" said Patrick, intrigued.

"Yes, they call themselves Anti-Hero because they believe you don't need to be a superhero to become a good manager. They are bold, offering an alternative to the traditional one-size-fits-all training programs."

"Interesting and quite unconventional. We always hear about the fact that we are all heroes and that the sky is the limit," said Patrick.

"I know! This message is appealing and makes you feel empowered, but it's also putting a lot of pressure on the managers. I am no hero. And when I see the number of planets and galaxies I have not yet visited in this 'Management' universe, it is paralysing. I'd rather stay on my couch and wait for things to get better by themselves."

"Thank you for sharing this with me. I do not feel alone anymore. By the way, what does an Anti-Hero Coach do differently then? What is so special about them?" asked Patrick.

"Well, they believe we are all different and there is no single path to becoming a good manager. One told me something interesting. He said because we have a hundred billion neurons and each neuron makes at least a thousand connections with other ones, if you were to do the maths, the probability of having the same links as someone else is none. And those neural networks define our individuality."

"Putting it this way, it sounds logical. And how would they help me on that path to become a better manager?"

"By helping you navigate this 'Management' universe. He is a co-pilot, a kind of tour guide for visiting galaxies like: The Qualities of a Good Manager, The Levers of Engagement, The Organisational Approaches, The Tools of a Good Manager, and a lot more."

"I never heard of those galaxies before. I am assuming you visited quite a few, didn't you?"

"Not that many. And some were more relevant than others. As an Anti-Hero Coach would say, it is not about visiting them all. That would be pointless. It is about visiting those that resonate with you. And the level of resonance with different planets depends on where you are in your personal and professional journey."

"But where should I start?"

"Let me introduce you to Reynold. He is an Anti-Hero Coach. He will answer your questions better than me."

"Sounds good. I really hope Reynold can help me; this is my last chance..."

"Come on Patrick, you'll be fine."

Graham organised for Patrick and Reynold to meet a few days later.

# 2

# *MEET WITH REYNOLD*

Patrick is a punctual person and he didn't want to wait, especially given that 'time was running out' for him and his team, he was quite eager to be done with it. Waiting for the Anti-Hero Coach made him agitated. At last, Reynold arrived:

"Hi, you must be Reynold, the Anti-Hero Coach I have heard so much about," said Patrick, accentuating the 'Anti-Hero' part with an amused expression on his face. He is not full of himself, but he has some sort of confidence and appears arrogant at times, although he thinks he is not, so it would seem to be unintentional.

"Yes, I am glad Graham recommended me. I am curious. Do you mind me asking what made you want to come here today to discuss with me?" asked Reynold.

"In a nutshell, I will lose my job if I don't turn the situation around with my team," said Patrick.

"Oh OK," said Reynold and then stayed silent.

"I must admit, I am desperate."

"What do you mean?"

"I really struggle to manage my colleagues to get the results we need."

"What do you mean by manage?"

"I suppose, I mean to make them be more efficient and autonomous."

"Do you believe you can change people?"

"I am not sure, but I am trying hard," said Patrick, laughing.

"OK, let me share something with you. The word 'manage' comes from the Italian 'maneggiare', in the sense 'put a horse through the paces of the manège'. And what do we still use with horses?"

"A whip and carrots, I guess..."

"That's right. What does this tell you?"

"That this is exactly what I do. But it does not work."

"Do you want me to share my definition?"

"Yes, please do."

"The etymology of 'Maneggiare' is derived from the Latin 'manus' meaning 'hand'. So, for me, the manager is the guiding force holding the baton of the orchestra conductor."

"I like it. It sounds nicer than the whip and the carrots. I must admit I ran out of carrots and the whip has done more damage than good."

"How does this make you feel?"

"Helpless and stressed. I don't look forward to going to the office every morning."

"What is the impact of this?"

"I am not in a great mood, and I usually shut the door. I guess it does not help."

"What else?"

"I don't sleep well, and I get angry too easily at home, which is not the type of Dad I want to be."

"How would you like the situation to be?"

"Well, I'd like to have good relationships with my team, being happy to work with them, getting the results, achieving our goals."

"What else?"

"Having less stress, sleeping well, and enjoying my time with my kids. Being more present."

"How would that make you feel?"

"Great, I'd feel more useful and satisfied. And I would still have a job," said Patrick with a smile.

"Is this something you would like to get some help with?"

"Absolutely!"

"I am assuming Graham told you a bit about how I work, did he?"

"Yes, he said you can assist me navigate this 'Management' universe. But if you could tell me more, that would be nice."

"That's right, I am helping managers to dare explore their own unique management style."

"Interesting. I am always up for a challenge."

"This is good. What else can I tell you? Ah yes, our mission. In a nutshell, we aim for managers to gain serenity while improving their team's performance."

"Sounds great. But why support managers in particular?"

"Have you heard about Gallup?"

"No."

"This is a renowned American analytics company. They conducted a survey showing that 70% of how engaged employees feel at work really comes down to how good and effective their managers are. I found out about this survey after reaching the same conclusion, when I interviewed senior managers and directors in my network."

"I see."

"So, are you ready to get started?"

"Yes! But where should we start?"

"I recommend we first explore planets within the galaxy close by, called 'The Qualities of a Good Manager'. This will make our trip more ecological. What do you think?"

"Looks excellent to me," answered Patrick enthusiastically.

"OK, in that case, let's go to my spacecraft. After you!"

Reynold had a spaceship coming straight out of Star Wars movies. Just like Boba Fett's ship, Slave I, it was a compact, crescent-shaped craft with a distinctive cockpit that rotated to keep the pilot upright during different flight modes.

They both jumped into the space vehicle and buckled up.

"Which planet would you prefer to explore first?" asked Reynold.

There was silence until Patrick hesitantly expressed: "Well, should we visit those planets in a specific order?"

"Not necessarily. Depending on your aversion to risk, you might decide to delve deeper into a planet you are already familiar with, or if you are looking for adventure, you would consider discovering one you have never heard of."

"Right, I see."

"Don't worry, there is no right or wrong choice with this type of expedition. I propose we reach the orbit of some planets and, whenever you feel inspired, just give me a shout and we can land."

"OK, let's do this!"

3

# *THE GALAXY OF THE QUALITIES OF A GOOD MANAGER*

3.1

# PLANET KINDNESS

As Patrick and Reynold approached Planet Kindness, the landscape unfolded into a breath-taking vista of perpetual spring. This mono-season planet radiates warmth and beauty, with flowers blooming in a kaleidoscope of colours under a sun that is always shining, but never too hot. This planet seemed to have been designed with harmony in mind, with buildings made of organic materials.

"What do you think, Patrick? Should we land and explore?" asked Reynold.

"Why not? I consider myself to be a kind person, but I am curious what they mean by kindness in this 'Management' universe," said Patrick.

"Alright then, let's prepare for landing. I see a friendly island in the form of a smile over there and there is a platform. Here we go."

Reynold had to stay in the spacecraft for some maintenance, so Patrick went on his own. He felt welcomed already. People were very polite and always with a cheerful expression. He could observe statues of Mahatma Gandhi with one of his famous quotes:

> *'The best way to find yourself is to lose yourself in the service of others.'*

Abhishek, an inhabitant, came to Patrick.

"What made you come to visit our lovely home?" asked Abhishek.

"I would like to figure out what kindness really means. But for now, I only have unanswered questions," said Patrick.

"What do you want to know?" asked Abhishek.

"Is it about being positive all the time, with a big smile, motivating the team: 'Keep on the good work!'? Would it mean that we need to be in control of our emotions to silence the negative? Is it about having genuine interest in others? Or could it be about allowing them space? Is this about helping a colleague who is in trouble and making a gesture? You see, lots of questions."

"What do **you** think?"

"It is very easy to be kind when all goes well, but when you have an employee who has poor performance or inappropriate behaviour, it becomes tricky."

"Right, and what do you do in that case?"

"I always try to keep my cool and make sure they don't take it the wrong way, but I still deliver the fact and it feels like a confrontation."

"What is the alternative?"

"I guess just letting it go."

"And what would that do?"

"Not much. The main issue here is that this employee would not know, and could not adjust or change anything."

"And would that be kind?"

"Hmm, I see your point. No, it would not. Giving feedback is essential to make any progress. But when they are negative, no matter how many precautions I take to deliver the message, some people would still react badly. This is not a kind gesture for them. They would rather you don't offer them your opinion. What should I do in that case?"

"You are correct. It is important to let your teammates know when they are mistaken. For example, if you are in a spaceship and see an asteroid in your path, it would be wise to tell the apprentice pilot to adjust the course, wouldn't it?"

Patrick nodded.

"And would it matter if the apprentice takes it right or wrong?" asked Abhishek.

Patrick shook his head.

"This case is extreme, but usually, not providing feedback would only delay the conversation and would most likely be worse. Also, does the failure of your teammates contribute to the mission's success?"

"No, it does not," said Patrick.

"And yet, failure is part of the learning process and you cannot avoid it. Sometimes, staying quiet is the best course of action. You cannot be on someone else's back and correct every move."

"I tried and I agree... You can lead a horse to water, but you can't force it to drink."

"You are funny, Patrick," said Reynold, laughing. "What I am saying is that you need to pick your battles and make a judgment call, given the situation."

"OK, it all makes sense. But it remains hard for me to deliver bad news."

"What are you afraid of?"

"To demotivate my team."

"What else?"

"That it would affect the atmosphere and other teammates."

"What else?"

"They won't like me anymore," said Patrick.

Abhishek stayed silent for a bit and then asked: "Is that so?"

"Not necessarily. I guess it is not justified. Thanks Abhishek!"

Patrick went back to join Reynold and they continued on the path. Someone gave them a leaflet. It was promoting an event about the Psychology of Altruism.

"We are in luck," said Reynold.

"Why is that?" asked Patrick.

"This is a great conference. Have you heard about the psychology of altruism?"

"No."

"Let's go then. It will be worth our time."

They both entered a roman-like temple and took a seat. The conference had already begun. The keynote speaker was called George C. Homans, a socialist who developed the Social Exchange Theory.

> *"Being kind has positive outcomes for both the receiver and the giver. It encourages both to be happier and contribute to their well-being. The motive seems to be based on expecting a return on that investment. Indeed, doing something nice to someone else builds up internal pressure on the receiving end, generating a social debt. Human relationships are formed by the use of a subjective cost-benefit analysis and the comparison of alternatives. We would, more or less consciously, make mental calculations to assess the rewards we receive against the costs we have to endure to balance it. This suggests that people are more likely to nurture connections that provide more benefits than drawbacks. Makes sense, doesn't it? Now, if you look at it from a manager's perspective, maintaining this debt with his team keeps*

*them engaged. However, this does not mean that a win-win relationship does not exist. Two individuals might feel indebted to each-other, each providing different values to the other and assessing those contributions differently. And in other relationships, both sides may find contentment, where everything is fair. Occasionally, there must be a necessity for a balancing act when one makes a gesture. As a result, the equation becomes unbalanced until it is reciprocated in some way. That would be boring otherwise..."*

George continued his presentation for another 30 minutes and there were a few other interesting speakers. At the end of the conference, while walking back to the spaceship. Reynold asked Patrick: "How did you find it?"

"Loved it."

"What part did you like the most?"

"The Ben Frankling Effect."

"Why is that?

"As you know, I prefer to be liked than not. If you were not pleasant to people, they would not hold you in high regard. They would not like you. So, it is natural for me to be kind. However, there is Fred, within my team, who hates my guts. He makes me anxious. I am walking on eggshells around him. The situation is very uncomfortable and, as a result, I don't like him in return."

"OK."

"So, if I understood this principle correctly, I would need to give a favour to Fred, make the first step. And by doing this, it would trick my mind into creating and nurturing the belief that I appreciate Fred. All of this is because my consciousness tries to justify its action."

"Interesting."

"Well, I am not sure I want to, but it is worth trying."

"What would be the impact of this?"

"If it makes me value Fred more, then I'd be happier to work with him. It would make things easier. I would be more comfortable around him. Also, it would create a social debt towards me. He might pay me back," said Patrick with a smile.

"What else?"

"I guess it would enhance the overall well-being of the team, giving them positive energy, allowing them to be more focused, more efficient."

"Would there be any unwanted impact?"

"Hmm. I don't see any. Worst case, it remains the same."

"Right."

"I can't wait to give this a try."

They arrived at the landing platform and entered the spaceship.

"Before we take off," said Reynold, comfortably seated, "I wanted to ask you. If there is one thing that you have learnt from this planet, what would it be?"

"I just need to accept not being perceived as a kind person from time to time," said Patrick.

"What do you mean, from time to time?"

"When it is important to stick with my opinion."

"OK, how do you find out when it is important to stick with your opinion?"

"For example, when I avoid conflict. This is not a right reason. Sometimes you must pick your battles, but you should not bypass them only because it is uncomfortable."

"Well spoken, Patrick!"

"Easier said than done."

"Indeed. I can see on the map that we are close to Planet Authenticity. Are you ready to depart?"

"Yes, let's go."

## QUESTIONS

What does kindness mean to you?

What small step could you take, that you have not already tried, to be a kinder manager?

What positive feedback did you not express yet to one of your colleagues?

## ADVICE & EXPERIMENTATION

Find something you genuinely respect for each of your colleagues and communicate it to them individually. It does not have to be related to performance. You could say, "I just wanted to tell you I appreciate your bluntness, even when it is about rejecting my ideas. I believe it brings valuable insights, so thank you."

I am sure you can find or create opportunities to be sincere and deliver this message of appreciation. Yes, it takes courage because it may sound awkward, especially if you never praise your colleagues, but it is worth it. People might initially perceive something is wrong with you, but deep inside, they love it. It cultivates good relationships.

3.2

# PLANET AUTHENTICITY

This planet experiences all four seasons with extreme weather. There is a mixture of high-tech, futuristic homes amongst simple huts. The landscape is colourful, but seems unplanned.

Once Reynold and Patrick landed, they walked towards the town centre. In this world, everyone expresses themselves freely through all aspects of life. Patrick is not too comfortable with some eccentricities. He is not used to people having no shame. Some of them were walking with no shoes and others were wearing socks with sandals.

"Finally," said Patrick.

"What?" said Reynold.

"Here, look, someone who looks sensible. I mean, according to my own standards."

"Excuse-me Madam, I am Patrick and I have just arrived with Reynold, my coach. I was wondering why this planet is called Planet Authenticity?"

"You need to ask Andrea. She is a disciple of Brené Brown, the well-known American researcher and storyteller. You will find Andrea in the Roman Amphitheatre near the high-tech building on the right."

"Oh OK, thank you. Have a good day."

On they went to a magnificent arena. Patrick loved those old buildings. He felt comfortable and safe. At this time, it was completely empty, apart from one person sitting in the first row.

"It should be Andrea!" said Patrick.

"You are probably right," said Reynold. "Shall we?"

Andrea was so focused on reading a book that she did not even hear them coming down the long stairs.

"Hi, someone told us you were the best person to ask a few questions about this world," said Patrick.

"Oh, I see. What do you want to know?"

"Please don't take it the wrong way, but people are eccentric here, nobody seems to follow any kind of norm yet it seems to be well accepted. How does it work?"

"Here you are in a safe space where everybody may express themselves freely. They don't have to play any role or conform to any standards."

"Does it imply people say what they think?"

"Come on Patrick, that would be too disturbing. It means they can be themselves."

"What do you mean by being themselves?"

"Let me ask you a question: who is Patrick?"

"This is very tricky. One could argue that I am my thoughts. Or that I am the results of my behaviours influenced by those same thoughts."

"OK, I suggest you add values, beliefs and emotions in the mix."

"I see. It is even more complex. How do you know who you are?"

"Let's put it this way: the more you seek answers about who you are, the more you would be yourself. It is a journey. One that never ends."

Someone on the other side of the amphitheatre waved at Andrea.

"Sorry guys, I must go. I hope you find out more about yourself during your stay," said Andrea.

"Yes, thank you," said Patrick, still trying to digest what Andrea had said.

Reynold and Patrick walked up the stairs silently. Once they arrived outside, Reynold asked Patrick: "Are you alright?"

"I am confused."

"What are you confused about?"

"I just don't know where to start."

"Right, you brought up behaviours, thoughts and she mentioned values, beliefs and emotions."

"Yes."

"Do you know what yours are?"

"I think so, even though I never asked myself this question. It requires a certain self-awareness."

"Sure enough. And what does authenticity mean to you?"

"For me, it is the reverse of playing games. I can't explain it, but I usually feel when someone is pretending, I receive mixed-messages."

"And what does this do to you?"

"I don't trust those people."

"Right, and do you play a role with your team?"

"Interesting. Hum... sort of. I am their manager, so I need to behave like a manager."

"What does that mean to you?"

"This will sound silly, but I want to show that I am superior in some ways, like I have to prove something."

Reynold remained silent for a bit then Patrick continued, "I suppose it is foolish. I imagine my team must see through this, me playing a role. I am the one sending them mixed-messages. No wonder they don't trust me."

"What do you want to do about it?"

"This needs to change. I need to figure this out. I have heard about the Planet Humility. It might be a good start. What do you think?"

"You are right. This planet is in this same galaxy."

On they went, back to the spaceship and took off towards Planet Humility.

## QUESTIONS

What aspects of your true self or personality have you not yet shared at work, and why?

What positive impact on your leadership or team dynamic did it have when you were authentic lately?

## ADVICE & EXPERIMENTATION

Have you tried 'Gradual Sharing' already? It is about starting with small, honest parts of your character or life that you are comfortable sharing with your colleagues. This might be as simple as discussing a hobby you're passionate about, an experience that shaped you, or your thoughts on a non-work-related topic. The key is to open up about things that matter to you, which invite others to do the same. This process enhances trust and can lead to a more cohesive atmosphere. It's about finding a balance between professionalism and personal connection.

3.3

# *PLANET HUMILITY*

When Patrick and Reynold got close enough, they recognised something looking like the Shire where the Hobbits live. It had a gentle landscape and low-lying hills. Patrick was a fan of the Lord of the Rings, so it was the first planet he was excited to visit. The climate seemed mild. It was a four-season planet but without extreme weather. Unlike the Hobbits, everyone wore simple uniform clothes.

Reynold, who knew this planet well, told Patrick to follow him. They went to the pub in the centre of the small town.

"Patrick, let me introduce you to Alfred, one of my oldest mates," said Reynold.

"What makes you come here, so far from your home, my friends?" asked Alfred.

"Patrick wants to change things with his team. He heard about your world and thought he may find some answers. Since you are the wisest man that I know of, your help would be much appreciated," said Reynold.

"Right, my wisdom tells me you could get us the next round while I have a chat with your friend," suggested Alfred, amused.

Reynold laughed and said: "Wise and smart. I am on it."

Reynold went to the bar to order some drinks.

"So, tell me Patrick. What do you think needs to change?"

"I am convinced I have the solutions to the problems my team brings to me. I am certain these solutions are the best. In fact, they have always worked when I was doing the job myself, but it no longer does. Maybe my methods do not provide the expected results anymore or they are not willing to do it my way. I am confused."

"What made you believe that humility would be a great ally as a manager?" asked Alfred.

"I just think I should accept that sometimes my solutions are not the best and that my team may have some that are worth considering."

"I see, and what would this do to accept you might be wrong?"

"It would make me more inclined to listen to my teammates."

"What else?"

"They would possibly come up with new ideas, different from mine. They don't look at the problem the same way, that's for sure. So their input could give me more insight."

"You are correct. It seems logical, doesn't it? Allow me to add to this that your team would bring some challenging points of view. This would allow you to gather intel and by weighing the relevance of it in an unbiased way, as much as you can, you would make more informed decisions."

"How are things going here?" Reynold asked, disrupting their conversation, bringing some refreshments.

"Thanks Reynold! We were talking about how a humble manager, by taking others' points of view into consideration, would improve their judgment," said Alfred.

"Right, I believe there are even more benefits to it. Let me tell you a story."

"So, where was I. Yes, when I was about 6 years old and would have dinner with my parents. Just like any other kids, my currency was attention. I did not know it then, but whether it was positive or negative attention, I would take it. I had two brothers and one sister, a decent size family. So, we had to fight for gaining recognition from our poor parents who tried their best to give as much to every one of their children. Anyway, on a good day, I would want to surprise them by clearing the table and putting dishes in the dishwasher. I knew they would be proud of me. Making a slight effort without even asking would go a long way. However, it would happen that before I had the chance to finish my dessert, my father, or my mother, would command me to do the same thing I planned on doing... My enthusiasm and spirit deflated instantly. I became reluctant. Do you understand why, Patrick?"

"You wanted to impress them, and they took that opportunity away from you."

"Yes, partly. But most importantly, it was not my idea anymore."

"OK, but what does it have to do with a humble manager?" asked Patrick.

"Well, even if you have the best solution as a manager, if you were to keep it for yourself and listen to your team, some might end up with the same conclusion. And as anybody, they would be happy that you chose their idea. It will make them more engaged. If my parents did not ask me to clear off the table, I would have done it with a smile on my face."

"Right, I get your point. But what about my authority and credibility as a manager?"

"I see where you are coming from. I understand that in most companies, managers are being promoted because they were the best in their function."

"Or they are good at politics," said Patrick, smiling.

Reynold laughed. "Yes, possibly, but this is not my point. It is difficult for those managers to let go of their expertise. Even if they still have some part of their job being operational. I believe being a manager is a role on its own and not another function. It requires a distinct skill set. You may have the best solutions and you can advise your team wearing the hat of the expert when required, but your goal as a manager is to develop your teammates. Give them the opportunity to explore their talent."

"OK, what you are suggesting here is that I start by asking them questions, hearing them out, guiding them towards a resolution, rather than giving them straight away my solution. Is that right?"

"That's a great way to do it. Do you want to try it?"

"Yes, but again, it is easier said than done. I am not the patient type."

"What could be the first tiny step? asked Reynold.

"Just forcing myself to ask at least one question."

"What would that be?"

"I don't know. It could be, 'Do you have any idea how to resolve this?', or something like this."

"OK, I suggest asking open questions to help them think. For example: 'What have you not tried yet?'"

"Sounds great," said Patrick.

"I see you are in good hands Patrick," said Alfred. "I wish you all the best on your journey. You are on the right track, and I am confident you will get your answers, those leading you to the next questions. Goodbye my friends. It is always a pleasure, Reynold."

While Alfred left the pub with Reynold and Patrick waving at him, saying goodbye, Patrick asked Reynold: "What did he mean by: 'those leading me to the next questions'?"

"Who knows," said Reynold.

After spending a few more days in an unsophisticated environment, and banging his head in the Hobbit's hut ceilings, Patrick considered it was time to continue the exploration, like Frodo did. Hopefully, it wouldn't be as bad for him.

Not long after they took off, they quickly found themselves in the orbit of Planet Assertiveness.

## QUESTIONS

What benefits would it bring to your company if your team was smarter than you?

What benefits would that bring you?

How would that make you feel?

What areas are individuals within your team stronger or more capable than you?

How might you encourage and tap into their strengths?

## ADVICE & EXPERIMENTATION

When you lead a meeting, try to be the last one to speak. By this, I mean you may start presenting or introducing a challenge or a project to your teammates. You could ask questions, of course. However, I suggest you keep your opinion as long as possible. That way, if someone has the same perspective as yours, assign this task to that person. They would be a lot more engaged. And they don't have to know you had the same idea. What are you trying to prove? Just leave them with 100% ownership.

3.4

# *PLANET ASSERTIVENESS*

Patrick had never heard of Planet Assertiveness. They could see small islands spaced out to prevent disturbance. Each of them looked very different, like factions. Buildings were quite distinct from one another. It took a while for Reynold and Patrick to find a spot to land. They needed to find an alternative. So, they left the ship in orbit and used the jet packs, which would make it easier to visit this world.

"How are you doing Patrick?" asked Reynold once they landed safely.

"I love those jetpacks! I got so much adrenaline! Feels good," said Patrick.

"I bet."

"Which island are we on?"

"I have no idea. There are so many islands on this planet."

"Why is that?"

"There are as many opinions as there are islands. People with the same beliefs and values stay together. They don't mix. It is a way for them to agree to disagree."

"That's sad."

"You think so? People seem fine here," said Reynold, pointing at children playing in a field.

There were a few parents on a bench watching out. Patrick determined to find out more, walk towards them.

"Hello, are these your kids?" asked Patrick to one parent.

"Yes, this is Pedro with the yellow T-shirt and Romuald over there."

"They are doing well! I am Patrick, by the way."

"Oscar."

"Do you mind if I ask you a few questions about your world?"

"No problem at all."

"I must admit, I did not know what assertiveness meant. I looked it up on Google and I am still confused. There are brackets straight after the word assertive like 'With respect' or 'Without being aggressive'. Why are there distinctions?"

"Is Google your Oracle?"

"You could say so, yes."

"I see. If there is one thing we all agree on across all the islands, it is the definition of assertiveness. Basically, we promote the idea of expressing one's opinion with confidence and self-assurance. However, and this is really important, one must deliver the message with care."

"What do you mean by delivering with care?"

"You don't have to be confrontational. And you better take other in consideration."

"Hm, why do you live on separate islands?"

"Simple, I would like to live in a certain way which is shared by the other inhabitants of this island. Elsewhere, they do things differently, which is fine. I won't impose my perspective on anyone."

"Right. It becomes easier to be assertive if you all agree."

"Yes, but we still are on the same planet. We have a lot of different bodies governing. We must work with each other from all islands."

"I see. I assume some people are better at being assertive than others. Like women, for example."

"What makes you think that?"

"It might be a prejudice of mine, but it is a message delivered with 'care' and this word is more associated with the female gender in my mind."

"It is exactly those biases that make it harder for them."

"I feel bad now."

"You are not the only one. Don't worry. Society expects them to be more nurturing and accommodating. These stereotypes can lead to negative perceptions of them. This means they must put in more effort to compensate. They have to show competence without compromising warmth."

Patrick's eyes were wide open, and he remained silent.

"It has a name, by the way: the 'double bind'," said Oscar.

"This is so unfair. Being assertive is hard enough," said Patrick.

"It depends on your personality. For some people, it comes naturally."

"And what about the others?"

"It is a skill they can develop."

"That's reassuring. Where would we start?"

"The first lesson we learn at school here is to look at things from your interlocutors' point of view, so you can adapt how you pass on your message. The most important thing is to be understood. Let me take another example. Pedro is only six years old and Romuald is fourteen. You don't talk to a child the same way as a teenager. This is how you take others into consideration."

"Interesting. Tell me more. What is the second lesson you learn at school here?"

It made Oscar want to laugh. "You are very curious. Good on you. This one takes a while for some people to integrate. Are you ready?"

"Sure"

"You must confront your fear of not being appreciated by someone."

"Oh, why is that?"

"What's your occupation?"

"I am a manager."

"So, your duty is to look after your team and your company, is that right? If something needs to be said for the benefit of the team or the company, whether colleagues approve of it, then this should be communicated."

"Sure, makes sense."

"I could go on with all the other lessons we learn at school, but it is dinner time for these two football players."

Patrick said goodbye to Oscar and went back to meet with Reynold, who had stayed close to the jetpacks.

"How did it go?" asked Reynold.

"Well, I have some work to do," said Patrick.

"Why is that?"

"As you know, it is difficult for me when people don't appreciate me. So, delivering bad news is not comfortable for me. Because I take others into consideration, I lose confidence and it makes me explain the whole context, going around in circles, not being clear, delaying the message."

"What could you do about this?"

"To be more direct."

"And how would you go about it?"

"I need to prepare for it. It would only take a minute to come up with a clear and concise speech."

"Awesome. May I share something with you?"

"Please do."

"I believe that, sometimes, it would not make a difference no matter what way you express yourself and how you say it. Some people cannot listen because another script is running in their head. The worst is that most of them are not aware of it. They believe their focus is laser-sharp, capturing every word you just uttered. But they don't, I assure you; I know what I am talking about! I used to be part of that club. You?"

"Sorry, can you repeat this please?" said Patrick, amused. "I am joking. I am definitely a member of this club at work."

"What about in our personal life?"

"Hmm, I will have to ask my wife..."

"Good idea. How about visiting another island?"

"I am not sure. I already have a lot to process."

"In that case, I suggest we return to the spaceship and visit Planet Empathy. How does that sound?"

"Intriguing, let's do this."

Patrick and Reynold put on their jetpacks again and returned to the spacecraft.

## QUESTIONS

Consider situations where you held back from being assertive. What stopped you? How might the outcome have changed if you had been more forthright?

Reflect on when others have been assertive and where that benefit you. How did you feel about that?

## ADVICE & EXPERIMENTATION

**Adjusting your volume of speech**, most people are at 3 out of 10. Try to get to 5 when you start a conversation, so it brings confidence in what you say.

You could also try **ending your sentence with a lower pitch** because a high pitch would bring doubt to the audience.

**Mirroring and matching.** If someone approaches you and speaks quietly (2 or 3 in volume of speech), try to match their level. This will build rapport and encourage them to talk more. Then, you can guide the conversation where you want it to go.

**Being concise**. Use declarative statements which are punchy and direct. As with anything, you need some training. Vinh Giang (Communication Skills Coach) suggests searching on Google: "Random Word

Generator", then make 10 declarative statements for each word generated.

3.5

# PLANET EMPATHY

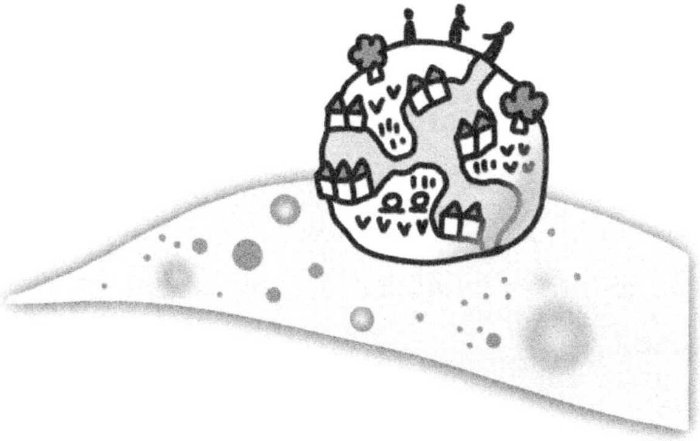

Planet Empathy is the most harmonious they have seen so far. You would notice interconnected landscapes as if they would accommodate each other. A really weird phenomenon is the weather. It is a microclimate everywhere, constantly changing and adapting to the inhabitants' needs. "A world that farmers would love," thought Patrick. While they were in orbit, he asked Reynold: "What is that dark area of the planet?"

"You'll find out soon enough."

Patrick remained silent for a few seconds and said: "Did you know empathy comes from Pathos in Ancient Greek? You would think I was a good student, but I am surprised I remember this. Anyway, it means 'to connect with another's emotions so profoundly that one experiences their pain as one's own'."

"This does not sound fun. How far would you be willing to go in empathy?" asked Reynold without allowing time for Patrick to respond. "Let me give you the definition of Jean Claude Ameisen, 'It is a window perpetually open onto the reflections that we perceive of others' inner worlds'. Not bad for a French doctor."

"Beautiful, indeed. Look over there, it's Andrea from Planet Authenticity." Patrick went towards her.

"What are you doing here?"

"For Brené Brown's conference. It was yesterday. Did you go?"

"No, we just arrived. What was it about?"

"She was talking about how to create a deep sense of connection with others. The idea to find the same feeling within yourself to comprehend the other person's emotion."

"I try to avoid these situations, to be honest, especially when someone tells me all about their difficulties, blah blah blah."

"I understand where you're coming from. It makes us vulnerable, that's tough. What's your strategy to avoid it?" asked Andrea.

"I try to help them look at the bright side, you know. Make it better."

"What do you mean?"

"For example, if one of my employees is getting too personal, telling me about their issues with their marriage falling apart. I'll just say: at least you have a marriage."

"Interesting. Brené mentioned this in her speech. She calls this to 'silverline'."

"And what would she say?"

"For her, whatever words we use, it does not make it better. It is more about the connection. You could tell them: 'I am not sure what to say right now, but I am glad you told me'."

"That's definitely not something I've said before. I am not very good at empathy."

"Don't worry, you are not alone. Have you heard about Gallup?"

"Yes, they do research –"

"They have the CliftonStrengths assessment. After 30 million completed it, they found out that only 18% have empathy in their top 5 strengths."

"Did you just 'silverline' it for me?" said Patrick, laughing.

"Good catch! I was testing you."

"What are the benefits of being an empathic manager, anyway?"

"The long list or the short list? Let's make it simple. Deeper connection, which builds trust and loyalty, and it is helpful to navigate conflict, because you now understand your colleagues' underlying emotions and needs."

"So, I would know them better and be able to influence them more easily then."

"Careful not to slip into the Dark Side of the Force."

"How so?"

"It is a no-go zone on this planet. We call those guys Dark Empath. They use empathy to manipulate people to their sole profits. Remember the Planet Authenticity; it needs to be genuine," Andrea said as she waved back at someone else. "This is my ride."

Patrick thanked her for those insights once again and returned to Reynold.

"So, Dark Empath, hey."

"That's right, do you want to meet some?" asked Reynold.

"I'll pass on that one."

"So, what did you get from your conversation with Andrea?"

"To be honest, I thought empathy was all about caring for people, but it is more about being present with them."

Reynold remained quiet.

Patrick continued: "Oh and empathy is costly, you have to be vulnerable, apparently."

"What do you mean by costly?"

"Courage. It takes courage."

"What do you want to do about it?"

"I may be brave enough, but some tools could help me with understanding my own emotions, though."

"Don't worry, it is part of the plan," said Reynold. "Are you ready to visit one last planet within this galaxy?"

"Always."

## QUESTIONS

Reflect on a time when someone genuinely understood you. What did the other person say or do that made you feel that way?

Consider a scenario where a team member is resistant to a new project approach. Instead of insisting on compliance, answer the question, "What's in it for them?"

## ADVICE & EXPERIMENTATION

When you are in a group conversation, pay attention to how people interact with each other, notice their body language, their facial expressions, their tone of voice. And because you are part of that discussion, only ask open questions or stay quiet. It will force you to not talk much and give you the time and focus to concentrate on the observation. This is another approach to listening.

Reflect what you've heard to ensure understanding, e.g., "What I'm hearing is..."

Validate their feeling with phrases like 'I can see why you would feel that way'.

**3.6**

# PLANET FAIRNESS

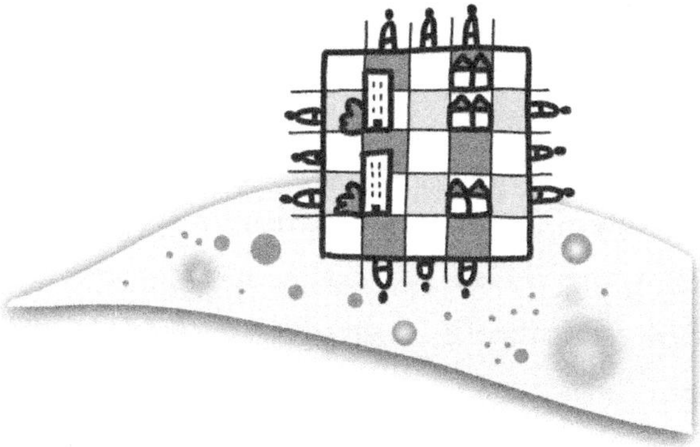

Planet Fairness is in a form of a square, meticulously organised. Different areas have distinct building types: small houses on a side and skyscrapers on another. One thing is certain is that there is a strict process for planning and construction. Everyone has to follow strict rules here.

Reynold and Patrick landed in a square with smaller houses and parks.

"This is going to be interesting," said Patrick.

"Why is that?"

"I believe fairness is impossible. We would already know it if life was fair."

"That's one way to look at it," said Reynold, smiling.

"I mean it. When I spend time with a colleague who needs help, another would feel left out. They interpret the same situation differently. I can't take everyone's perspective into consideration, it's just impossible."

"Let me introduce you to Justine. She is part of the THEMIS program. It manages their voting system."

Reynold walked towards a small house. Patrick was surprised as he expected her to work in one of the massive towers on the next square area.

"This is her home. She knows you are coming for tea."

Patrick went by himself to the doorstep and knocked.

"Welcome to my remote office!" said Justine.

A massive transparent interface stood in the middle of the main room. She was moving apps with her hands as in the Minority Report movie.

"What is that?" said Patrick.

"THEMIS, it receives all the laws for which people have to vote. It calculates who the law affects and sends them a report and a voting link. Everyone has their say."

"Impressive."

"Reynold told me you don't believe in fairness. It's a tricky one, isn't it?"

"If I can figure it out, I might stop my kid from yelling 'it's not fair' all the time."

"Why is that?"

"Don't you have kids?"

"Not yet."

"I have twins, Daniel and Timothy. One does not listen much, and the other seems to learn from his brother's mistakes. Daniel would never put his jacket on the hanger nor his shoes on the rack when getting back home. It makes me so angry. I repeat it to him all the time. I would punish him, of course."

"Fair enough."

"Yes, but when Timothy, once in a while, would do the same. Because he is tired or whatever. I would let it slip. Because I know it is a one-off. But then, Daniel would cry out loud, 'it's not fair, why is he not punished'."

"What's the rule?"

"Well, to clear out their gear when coming back home."

"What if they don't?"

"At some point, I punish them."

"Do you want my opinion on this?"

"Yes," said Patrick hesitantly.

"The rule is not clear. So, it cannot be fair."

"What do you mean?"

"Your kids are unaware of whether or when they will face reprimands. If the guideline was to allow for two reminders, then David would understand why his brother was off the hook this time."

"So, clear rules and consistent enforcement equals fairness, is that it?"

"Let's say that it contributes to it. For you as a manager, it's also about measuring performance against the same standards for everyone to have the same chance," said Justine, while manipulating screens on her see-through display, "Here, look!"

*According to a survey conducted by Harvard Business Review, researchers discovered that only 18% of individuals believe their work environment is highly fair.*

"That's not a lot. I wonder if my team is part of this group... And what's the benefits of being a fair manager?"

Justine moved her finger so as to scroll down and it displayed:

*The perceptions of a more equitable experience improve employee performance by up to 26% and retention by up to 27%.*

"Now you're talking! Does that mean Daniel will follow the rules 26% of the time?" said Patrick, amused.

Patrick greeted Justine and left her home office thinking how outstanding it would be to have the same interface for himself. He found Reynold having a nap on a bench in a neat communal garden.

"How did it go?" asked Reynold.

"I have some work to do. I need to structure a bit more the performance criteria of my team and update the code of conduct, but more importantly, to stick to it."

"Consistency! I'm glad you have a plan of action already. Let's continue our conversation on the ship. We have a long way to reach the next galaxy."

Patrick and Reynold went back to the square landing zone and retrieved the spacecraft.

## QUESTIONS

Reflect on times when you've felt unfairly treated. What would have made those situations seem fairer to you?

How can you apply those insights to your management style?

## ADVICE & EXPERIMENTATION

To promote fairness within your department, I suggest you pick one benefit that your company is offering to employees. Then find an opportunity during a meeting to explain how this advantage addresses the needs of the teammates, acknowledging their difference about their potential challenges. If we take the example of a 'flexitime' (a working schedule which allows employees to choose when to start and end their workday), you might remind them this is not only for parents to spend more time with their children, which is great by the way, but also for those who pursue a dream to climb Mount Everest and get to train more often. If you are up for it, it would be an excellent bonding experience to ask those who want to share how they (would) use that extra spare energy and how beneficial it is to them.

**3.7**

# SOMEWHERE IN THE COSMOS

On their way towards another galaxy, Patrick was contemplating the cosmos. He found it fascinating.

"Is it always like this with other managers you help on their journey?"

"Every time is different," replied Reynold, his Anti-Hero Coach.

"What do you mean?"

"Each time, it's a distinct itinerary, visiting various planets and galaxies. Some visit just one galaxy. Others explore many, but not extensively."

"It was quite the ride."

"What did you get out of this Galaxy of the Qualities of a Good Manager?"

"I understand now how these qualities are useful to engage my team. It was great to clarify them, though. And see how I could develop some based on my context."

"You are raising an important point. Some are more valuable than others depending on your environment. I believe a good manager knows which trait of his own to exhibit according to the situation."

"I am assuming it is also about trying to develop as many of those qualities as possible, isn't it?"

"Not necessarily, but it's important to recognise which quality would be useful to integrate. By this, I mean there are countless ways to express those qualities. The challenge is to try different approaches to find your own way, to find what works for you."

"Makes sense."

"I see you made a list of your lessons learned here. Is that right?"

Patrick nodded and showed it to Reynold.

***Planet Kindness:*** *Not be afraid to provide bad news/feedback, let them learn and grow.*

***Planet Authenticity:*** *Stop playing a role to build trust.*

**Planet Humility**: *Stop providing a solution straight away. First, ask questions to engage.*

**Planet Assertiveness**: *It's OK if you are not appreciated sometimes. You can't please eve-ryone.*

**Planet Empathy:** *Being present to create a deeper connection.*

**Planet Fairness**: *Clear rules*

"Good stuff. Are you ready for the next galaxy of the Organisational Approaches?"

"Yes. I should know, but what are those?"

"It's how a company organises and plans its work to get things done efficiently."

Patrick nodded.

"You'll find this one quite impressive too, with many planets. I suggest we explore only a few to start with. We can always come back later. We are nearly there."

4

# *THE GALAXY OF THE ORGANISATIONAL APPROACHES*

# 4.1

# PLANET PALO ALTO SYSTEMIC

Patrick and Reynold arrived in the orbit of the Planet Palo Alto Systemic. Patrick had seen nothing like this. It was another odd planet, resembling a spherical Rubik's Cube. The landscape was dynamic, constantly shifting. Reynold explained rotations occur when inhabitants affect their physical environment too much or when there are social imbalances. It is an ever-changing mosaic illustrating circular causality. Once they landed, Reynold got the jetpacks out.

"What are you doing?" asked Patrick.

"We might need them to retrieve the ship if a rotation happens. Let's head to the Mental Research Institute, the MRI. This is where Paul Watzlawick worked in Communication Theory, understanding human interactions."

They both arrived near the building.

"I expected something bigger," said Patrick.

"Don't judge by the size of it. They are major players in the development of modern therapeutic practices. Let me introduce you to Greg."

Greg was in the restaurant area, having coffee.

"Oh visitors! We usually have patients here. What can I do for you?"

"I'd like to know more about the systemic approach," asked Patrick.

"It's a paradigm. We believe we are in a relational world, an interconnected system. There are 4 principles. My favourite is the 'Circular Causality'. Each action influences the next in a continuous loop, where everyone's behaviour affects and is affected by others."

Patrick seemed a bit confused.

"Let's take an example. Do you have conflicting interactions sometimes? A recurring one, maybe?" asked Greg.

"With my son, Daniel, when he does not put his jacket on the hanger," said Patrick.

"Very annoying, indeed. Describe it to me. What happens at the very beginning of the interaction?"

"I open the door, let my kids in and Daniel would run and drop his jacket on the floor, ignoring me."

"What makes you interpret that?"

"He does not look at me, rushing to his toys."

"What do you feel when he does this?"

"Not respected."

"And in terms of emotion?"

"Anger."

"What are the reasons you want him to follow this rule?"

"I prefer when things are tidy. I can think more clearly and discipline is important to me. I'd like to teach him."

"What do you believe is going on in his mind?"

"I guess he doesn't care. He might hear me in the background, but his excitement takes over."

"What happens next?"

"I would repeat myself, louder and louder and eventually come to him, grab his toy until he does what I've asked him to do. Then he would complain, cry and slam doors on his way."

"What results from this?"

"I am even more upset. His jacket is still on the floor. Nobody's happy."

"Right. Thank you for sharing this. So, the principle of circular causality, in contrast to simple cause-and-effect, is that your emotions and actions are feeding off each other in a loop. His actions influence your reactions, and your reactions, in turn, influence his actions, creating a cycle that just keeps going."

Suddenly, they felt the ground shaking like a mild earthquake.

"What's happening?" asked Patrick.

"We just rotated. Second time this year."

"How often does this happen?"

"It used to be once every three to five years, but it has been speeding up in the last decade. Sorry, guys, I need to make sure everything is OK with my family."

Greg took his briefcase and left the building in a hurry.

"We better check on our vessel," said Reynold.

On this occasion, Reynold and Patrick were lucky. The rotation did not move their spaceship further away.

"It is not a good time to be around. It usually causes some crisis. Let's take off," said Reynold.

Once they were back in space, Patrick started the discussion, "I am a bit frustrated. I understand the principle of circular causality, but I'm still struggling to grasp how it helps."

"Our brain is wired to predict. You proved it by telling the story of what happens in that chain of action/reaction with your son. Every time, it reinforces this interaction pattern, it reassures both of you. You find it less stressful when you know the outcome, even if not favourable."

"This is so stupid."

"I would argue it is very smart, but I understand what you are trying to say. Now, there is a way to hack this pattern. You need to change your behaviour."

"What do you mean?"

"What can you do differently?"

"I could try to keep cool and leave him a few minutes with his toys first."

"Interesting. You could also adjust your tone of voice or joke about it. The point is, you would send a different message to Daniel, and he's likely to react in a new way."

"My challenge will be to contain my frustration."

"I can't wait to visit Planet Emotional Management with you. But it is in the next galaxy. I suggest we explore another few planets here first. How about Planet Servant Leadership?"

"Never heard of it."

## QUESTIONS

What are the recurring interactions with your team (or a particular colleague) that you would like to change?

Now that you have identified those situations, what would you do differently to get a different response?

If you think you tried quite a few things already, what have you not dared trying yet?

## ADVICE & EXPERIMENTATION

Celebrate diverse paths to goals. Recognise the various ways team members achieve their objectives, reinforcing the principle of equifinality (one of the other 4 principles). Even more powerful, you could just ask them examples of situations where they were proud of achieving a goal their way, and how they did it.

It's a great technique to show the value of diverse problem-solving strategies and to foster an inclusive environment. It is also likely to inspire others to gain confidence in trying different approaches.

4.2

# *PLANET SERVANT LEADERSHIP*

Planet Servant Leadership is one of the most fertile, to sustain life. Pathways can be seen everywhere, to facilitate people journeying together between hubs. These were gigantic constructions distributing resources and providing guidance to the citizens. Most other buildings were modular. Inhabitants could configure them based on their needs.

After Reynold and Patrick landed on this planet, they found themselves in a new coffee shop. There were only round tables that made everyone see each other and promoted collaboration. Customers moved chairs and tables at their convenience.

As part of the opening event of his café, the owner had organised a silly contest, inspired from the TV game show 'Hot Ones', which was to taste the 10 hot sauces from mild (1.700 Scoville level) to crazy hot (2.6 million). The 'garçon de café' came in and said, "We've had no winners today so far. Here are your chicken wings to pour some hot sauce on. Now, what would you like to help with the burning sensation? Water? Ice cream? Honey? Milk?"

Patrick looked at Reynold to find answers.

"I think milk would be great, thanks," said Reynold.

"No problem. If you need anything, just shout, I will be right behind the bar. Oh, and please stop when it feels too much. Your health is our priority."

Patrick liked hot sauce, but his body was not cooperating. They started easily with the first three.

"So far so good," said Patrick, "Hang on, this one is sneaky."

"Yes, I call it the two-stage burn," said Reynold.

"So, tell me, the name of this planet is quite self-explanatory. I guess the lesson would be for managers to serve their team, isn't it?"

"It is more about the managers' duty of ensuring the well-being and development of their teams."

Patrick nodded and said, "I like the names!" while pointing at bottle seven, eight, and nine.

*'Unwavering Inferno': a steady and intense heat that mirrors deep commitment.*

*'Righteous Blaze': a pure and honourable warmth, reflecting moral integrity.*

*'Phoenix Flame': Rises from its ashes, embodies transformation and positive change.*

"These are key guidelines on this planet. The result is what you get from the hottest sauce," said Reynold, pointing at the last bottle.

*'Trust Forge': an unyielding and scorching fire that forges lasting bonds, capturing the strength and resilience of trust.*

"Does it make your mouth become a forge?" said Patrick, laughing.

"We'll find out soon enough!"

Patrick grabbed the hottest sauce, 'Trust Forge,' and smiled. "I think I get it now. In order to forge trust," he said, holding up the bottle, "it takes commitment, integrity, and giving space to grow," he continued, pointing at the other bottles.

The 'garçon de café' overheard the conversation while coming towards their table, and said, "This is General George Patton's favourite!"

"Who is this General?" asked Patrick.

"He commanded the Seventh United States Army in the Mediterranean. He played a critical role in World War II on Earth," said Reynold.

"Indeed, and his famous quote is on our menu here," said the 'garçon de café', showing 'la carte' and then disappearing behind the bar again.

*Never tell people HOW to do things. Tell them WHAT to do and they will surprise you with their ingenuity.*

Patrick's eyes widened as the realisation hit him, a brief spark of understanding flashing across his face.

"Yeah, this is a hot one," said Reynold.

"No, it's not the sauce. I just made the connection to my experience on Planet Humility, where I committed to asking open-ended questions before offering my solutions."

"What about it?"

"Now I realise the missing ingredient—it's for me to let go and trust my team to figure out the *HOW*. This should also help my team with creativity."

"Talking about this..." said Reynold, pointing to the fourth bottle.

*'Ignite Spark': A vibrant and unpredictable heat that fuels innovation and surges of creativity.*

"This is already getting far too hot for me. I am all sweaty, my throat is hurting like hell, and I can't feel my tongue anymore," said Patrick.

Reynold burst into laughter and said, "You did not touch your milk!"

"I don't drink milk. Talking about it, I am eager to return to the Milky-Way and change a few things at work."

"We can. I suggest while we are here to visit one last world within this galaxy. It is only a few minutes away, very close by. It will help you get over the hot sauces, I promise."

"OK then."

## QUESTIONS

What current project could you let go of some control from?

What are the risks implied?

What would be the worst-case scenario?

What might you do to minimise these uncertainties while surrendering a bit of control?

## ADVICE & EXPERIMENTATION

Act as a pivotal resource for your team, signifying that their success is your utmost priority. A simple, yet profound way to manifest this support is by regularly inquiring, "How can I assist you in achieving, or even surpassing your goals?" This approach not only underscores your commitment to their growth, but also opens avenues for meaningful dialogue and mutual progress.

4.3

# PLANET LIBERATED COMPANY

Patrick and Reynold could see Planet Liberated Company even before they took off from the Planet Servant Leadership, like the moon to earth. As they got closer and closer, the two spheres looked very similar. The major distinctions they could observe were the absence of hubs and moving pathways on the next world. However, there was the same richness in nutrients and resources and the same modular buildings.

They landed close to a billboard where there was an ad about a pub which had opened recently. There was a karaoke contest specifically organised for the opening event.

"This should let you forget about the hot sauce, don't you think?" said Reynold.

"I'm not so sure. I still feel dizzy."

"It must be over there. I can see some lights."

"I can't find any pathways, though."

"Trust me, just walk, go ahead."

At that moment, something magical happened - a pathway formed in front of Patrick's steps.

"Amazing!"

After a few minutes, they arrived at the pub, which had round tables, the same as the coffee shop on the previous planet.

"Welcome gentleman, I'm Rose. I will look after you to make sure you have a great evening. Tonight is Karaoke night. We start in a few minutes. Help yourself, find a seat, anywhere you like."

The place was packed. Reynold and Patrick struggled to find a table. Soon after, Rose took the mic and said, "Thank you everyone for coming. Let's split up into 3 groups. One group is to decide the success criteria for the winners, another the theme and the last the prizes."

"So, this is a contest the contestants organise," said Patrick privately.

"There is no top-down structure here. There are not even job titles in their business world," said Reynold.

Patrick seemed surprised and intrigued.

"Some companies on Earth use this approach. FAVI for example. Their CEO, Jean-François Zobrist, believes treating employees like adults, capable of making their own decisions, is the way forward," said Reynold.

"What chaos it must be."

"They are not the only ones. Gore-Tex and Patagonia in the US have implemented elements of it. They all get outstanding performance, more engagement, and innovation too."

"I really struggle to see how this works. You need to put all your faith in your team."

Rose arrived at their table and asked, "How is everything?"

"May I ask you a question? How does your society function without hierarchical organisation?"

"Let's use the analogy of music. Take the traditional orchestras - musicians strictly follow the conductor's lead and sheet music. It is very precise. Now, take a jazz ensemble. It thrives on improvisation. While there is a basic structure and tune like teams' responsibilities, company goals and values, they can improvise and express their unique talents."

"Interesting," said Patrick.

"Did you guys join a group yet?"

"Yes, we are helping to decide the success criteria," said Reynold.

They joined a group of 10 people. One, called John, stepped up to facilitate the decision to be made. He was asking a lot of questions like, "What criteria should we take into consideration?" and people answered, 'Voice quality', 'Presence', 'Interpretation', 'Audience Engagement'. Then "How would we assess against those criteria?" and people suggested some ideas until Patrick said, "Why don't we elect three judges for the first three criteria, one for each? And use the crowd's response for Audience engagement."

Everybody agreed with Patrick's suggestion.

They then figured out the scoring approach and the different phases of the Qualifications, Semi-finals and Final.

"How do we figure out who qualified?" asked John.

"I suggest a minimum of 75% score on three out of the four criteria," said Reynold.

They all nodded in approval.

All groups communicated their decisions to Rose, who shared the rules with everyone, and the contest began.

While listening to some painful contestants, Patrick asked Reynold, "I am still trying to figure this out. Does it mean a salesperson would set his own goals?"

"That's right."

"It sounds too easy."

"Let's look at the advantages of this approach. What do you think they would be?"

"It would be more realistic, as they should know better what they feel they can achieve or not."

"What else?"

"It is engaging. They would become more motivated and take ownership. I see your point, but what if the goal is too low for the company, paying wages or financing expansion plans?"

"This is a great opportunity for collaboration and understanding the reasons; to think about ways to improve, provide training, more incentives."

"So, if I get this right, it allows a conversation beforehand to address it, rather than discussing after the fact, where the salesperson did not achieve the arbitrary goals set for them."

"That's one way to look at it."

"How do organisations implement this shift?"

"It depends on their size, and risk tolerance too. Some would run a pilot, or partial implementation, gradual transition -"

"I think this is your turn, Reynold. 'Queen', 'We are the champions'. Good luck!"

Unfortunately, Reynold did not qualify. To be fair, the judges set the bar high. He returned to his place, exhausted, but with a smile.

"I believe it is time to go back home now. I can't wait to make some changes at the office, and the clock is ticking," said Patrick.

"Are you chickening out?"

"I just don't want to steal the show," said Patrick, laughing.

"Come on, let's see what you've got!"

"Alright, but we get out of here as soon as it finishes."

"Of course. The ship is ready. Have some fun."

Patrick went to sing 'Eye of the tiger' by 'Survivor'. He qualified, by only a few points, but then lost after singing 'Don't Stop Believin' by Journey at the semi-final. They both had a great time and watched the final before heading back to the spacecraft.

## QUESTIONS

What are your beliefs regarding employees being responsible adults?

What could you do as a small step to try this approach?

Which department or project might be a good prospect to get its own freedom and autonomy?

Which colleagues would you pick for trying this out?

How would you measure the success of it?

## ADVICE & EXPERIMENTATION

Encourage your teammates to experiment and innovate boldly within their roles, embracing both their triumphs and the valuable lessons hidden in setbacks. Consider launching a 'Fail Forward' initiative, inspired by John C. Maxwell, where team members openly share their experimental journeys, outcomes, and insights during a monthly gathering. This approach not only demystifies failure, making it an expected step in the learning process, but also spotlights the importance on innovative thinking.

4.4

# TIME OUT ON PLANET EARTH - MILKY WAY

Straight after they landed on Planet Earth, Patrick headed determinedly to his office for the Kick-off meeting of the day. Meanwhile, Reynold met with other Anti-Hero Coaches for a coaching supervision session.

"Morning everyone," said Patrick. "As you know, we are on the board's radar, as we have not been performing lately. We need to get better and become profitable within the next 6 months. Any idea on HOW we can achieve this?"

The impression made by General Patton seems to have motivated him enough to put it into action. Most of his team came up with new ideas, some that Patrick considered more or less interesting. He took a leap of faith and gave them a wild card on the How (how to do their work) and plan on re-assessing the results within 3 months. He also asked them: "How may I help you with that?" Despite their limited financial resources, he believed they could find innovative ways to reallocate the budget by pausing other projects. Or he might offer his time and support to those who needed assistance.

It was challenging for Patrick to let go of control. Not that the ideas and suggestions that his team provided were ridiculous, but he would not have done it this way. So, he called Reynold on his mobile.

"Hey coach, I am finding this quite difficult. This is a huge gamble I am making with going with their solutions," said Patrick.

"OK."

"I mean, the chances of failure are really high."

"What risks are you taking?"

"My reputation for one, my job, their jobs too."

"I see. What is the cost of not doing anything?"

"Hmm. If we continue like that... Get fired."

Patrick went quiet for a few seconds, and then said, "Looking at this from this angle, I guess the risk of implementing their solutions is not that bad after all. I have nothing more to lose, anyway. Worst case, we end up with the same results as taking no action."

Reynold nodded.

Patrick added, "It does not simplify things or provide any comfort. I mean, this is reassuring and gives me confidence in continuing that course, but I hate the sensation. First, I believe there is a high probability of not being successful. Secondly, if their plan works..." Patrick pauses, realising something, "Well, what does this make of me?"

"What does it make of you?"

"Yes, what impression would my colleague have of me? If my ideas are not the best anymore, this puts my competence in question here."

"What other way could you look at it?"

"Hm. I guess it is a kind of solution of its own to let them work how they want to."

Patrick fell silent once more for a few seconds and said, "OK. I suppose I should not change course now, and give it a chance, but again, it is difficult."

"What do you mean?"

"It's stressing me out. I am a bit on edge. Afraid too."

"What do you feel in your body?"

"Sensations in my neck and shoulders. Tensions."

"Where else?"

"Not sure. Sometimes in my belly too."

Reynold stayed silent to let Patrick experience those feelings.

After what seemed like a long silence, Patrick said, "I need to deal with this. It would be great to use some practical resources to support me. I remember you mentioned the Galaxy of the Tools of a Good Manager. Should we go there and check this one out? I have no time to waste."

"That's what I call a quick break!"

Off they ventured back to the deep dark universe towards this other galaxy. Reynold set the ship's navigation control for Planet Emotional Management.

5

# *THE GALAXY OF THE TOOLS OF A GOOD MANAGER*

5.1

# *PLANET EMOTIONAL MANAGEMENT*

After a long trip through space, Patrick and Reynold arrived on Planet Emotional Management. It was the utopia of the Zen world, with serene temples promoting mindfulness and expansive gardens with flowing streams and tranquil pond. But some areas were darker and chaotic, with ruins, unkempt landscapes, twisted trees and turbulent waters. Our fellow visitors landed on a more welcoming area and waited in a temple to participate in a meditation class for beginners.

"Welcome to my sanctuary," said Aïsha, the Mindfullness Coach. She added, "What is self-awareness to you?"

Patrick, very excited, raised his hands and said, "Well, to the extreme, I would say to be aware of all the signals received through our body. Through our skin, our joints, our muscles, our fascia, our brain, our neurons, our sympathetic and parasympathetic system, our biochemistry, our hormones, our DNA... It would mean to be conscious of our unconscious..."

"I am not sure we could consciously handle that much information," said Aïsha, laughing, and added, "Someone else?"

"To be aware of our own thoughts, our emotions," said another participant.

"Yes, and in what situation would it be beneficial?"

"When things go wrong," said Patrick.

"Why is that?" said Aïsha.

"Then I could have some sort of control over how I should act, rather than expressing the powerful emotions, and then regret it."

"Right. Do you have a specific example?"

"Yes, I have loads. One was a few months ago. In the morning, I was at home getting ready to go to the office. It started when my car keys were missing. I looked everywhere, no luck. I thought I may have left it inside it. It would not be the first time. But then, I could not find my car. A thief stole it. I called the police while trying to catch a bus. I took the bus, and someone became sick and vomited. I could not bear it, so I moved out of the bus and walked. I got a call back from the cops saying they had found the vehicle. I was relieved for a second, and then they said it was burnt... I eventually arrived at my workplace and made a presentation, but my head was too busy with what just happened."

All participants looked at him with a mix of surprise and sympathy.

"What a day!" said Aïsha.

"What should I do in that case? Should I have cancelled the meeting? Should I have informed them about the situation?"

"I see, so all the emotions of that morning were still resonating within you during the presentation."

"Yes."

"Could you name those?"

"Anxiety, surprise, disappointment, frustration, disgust, anger."

"OK, and if you had been more self-aware, what would you have done?"

"I guess I would have taken a bit more time. I was already late anyway, a minute more, a minute less..."

"What for?"

"To just relax and breathe."

"And what would this do?"

"I would have been the manager they expected that morning, to be more inspiring and energetic."

"Very good. Let me explain to you all, 'The chimp paradox', a book by Professor Steve Peters, an English psychiatrist who worked with elite athletes. The author describes the mind management model, which divides the brain into 3 parts. The Human, being the rational part, the Chimp, being the emotional machine, reacting impulsively and the Computer, storing useful information and habits. I will show you how to work with your Chimp Mind. Before it expresses itself and lashes out to the world, you will gain the opportunity and space for your Human

Mind to reflect on what would be the best course of action, rather than having your default reaction. Questions so far?"

Everybody shook their heads, all clear.

"Let's start then with our meditation. Make yourself comfortable and close your eyes. Take three deep breaths. Focus on your surroundings, noise, and smell. Now concentrate on your breathing, in and out. Observe your thoughts and let them go. It's OK if the Chimp Mind takes over. We are only human. When and if you catch it, just return to your breath."

Once the meditation finished, Patrick and Reynold walked around a dark area and entered another temple. They attended a training session of journaling with a coach guiding them with formulating questions.

Then they moved on to a massive tent a few yards away. There was a big sign at the entrance: 'Silent Retreat'.

"What do you think, Patrick?" asked Reynold.

"I am here to experiment. It might help soothing the Chimp Mind..."

"Well done, great attitude."

Patrick stayed for about four days and could not take it anymore. Reynold came out to follow him.

They walked back toward the spacecraft and started debriefing.

"How did it go?" asked Reynold.

"I thought it would tranquillise the Chimp Mind, but it was worst for a time and then it softens a bit. It was an interesting experience. Man, it is so good to talk right now," said Patrick.

"What did you learn from this planet?"

"This is a new world for me. I was aware these people existed, but to witness some of what they are doing was insightful. I learnt some activities were easier for me to practice than others."

"If there was one activity you would want to engage in as a routine, what would it be?"

"Journaling, 100%."

"OK", said Reynold and then remained silent.

"Taking time out and writing things down, for me, makes it real. I put words on those feelings. I also better understand what situations generate what emotions. It does not explain the reasons those events trigger me. But I can recognise it more often when it happens."

"Is this something you want to do?"

"Yes, definitely."

"When would you like to start?"

"Today."

"Great. When is a good time for journaling for you?"

"Before I go to bed, when the kids are asleep, and all the chores are done."

"Where would that be?"

"In my office, so I am alone and at a desk."

"OK, what could get in your way?"

"When I come back home late in the evening, when I have tennis on Wednesdays, but that is only once a week. It should be fine."

"It should be fine?"

"Well, not really. I know this has been a problem for me in the past. If I skipped once, then it fell through."

"What have you not tried yet to get over this?"

"I guess I need to schedule this in my diary. I make sure I do what I planned on there."

"Fantastic, Patrick. You seem to have found a great tool to help you navigate this challenging period. Where should we go now?"

"I saw the Planet Love on the way, and I wonder what this one is doing in this Management universe."

They buckled up and started their route towards this next world.

## QUESTIONS

Which emotions challenge you the most, and why?

Where in your body do you feel them arise?

## ADVICE & EXPERIMENTATION

You may consider:

- Accepting the Chimp Mind will have the best of you from time to time.
- Embracing the moments when it dominates you is key.
- Resisting only feeds its strength.

One way to do this is by journaling daily about your experiences, especially on those occasions of impulse, so it helps in understanding their origins. This practice isn't just about acceptance; it's a step towards personal growth and enhancing your emotional intelligence.

5.2

# PLANET LOVE

On this planet, the landscapes are diverse and rich, with beautiful gardens and buildings, or better described as innovative structures. People seemed focused and there was an energising midst in the atmosphere, like a life-enhancing gas that boosts creativity, joy and enthusiasm.

Patrick and Reynold landed on an open field where inhabitants were doing outdoor activities. As soon as they disembarked from their spaceship, they could hear music and laughter. Patrick felt a positive sensation but was not sure what.

"I suggest we visit the Mayo Clinic hospital. They have a fantastic research centre. A friend of mine works there - he is a Love Doctor," said Reynold.

"A Love Doctor! What a marvellous job! I'll follow your lead," said Patrick.

"We need to take the fast train over there," said Reynold, pointing to a decent size building with futurist architecture.

The train was very spacious. There was no noise and an agreeable smell. They arrived at their station and walked a few minutes to get to a well-designed building with curves. It was a high rise with flowers all around. They entered the building and went to meet with Colin. After reuniting with warm embraces, Reynold explained to Colin the questioning of Patrick about the location of this planet.

"I understand you expected this planet in the Galaxy of the Qualities of a Good Manager, with managers showing love to their team. But it is more about managers helping their teammates find what they love doing," said Colin.

"Interesting. And how do we do this?" asked Patrick.

"We found out those spending less than 20% of their time on the activity that is most meaningful to them had higher rates of burnout. It means it helps us cope with the other activities we are not too passionate about."

"So, is this to avoid burnout?"

"Not only. I recommend you read 'Love + Work' by Marcus Buckingham. The author refers to the ADP Research institute's data on engagement. It shows that employees are far more likely to be productive too."

"What you are saying is if I were to let my team do whatever they love doing at work for a day a week, we would get better results."

"Yes."

"Being in the service industry where time is money, I don't see how this would be possible for us."

"What activity could your teammates be passionate about that would be billable to your clients?" asked Reynold.

"Hmm, I did not see it this way. I thought only research time or training would be things they enjoy. I guess I need to find out, but how?" said Patrick.

"One way is to uncover the pace at which your teammates learn something new, doing a new activity. The faster they learn, the more likely the activity brings them joy. It is all about letting them explore and having experiences to discover what they love," said Colin.

Patrick nodded and then looked around and continued, "I feel something different since we got here. Do you feel it too, Reynold?"

Colin smiled and said, "We have a mysterious element in our atmosphere. It alters your consciousness."

"That's why my head is a lot quieter. I can think more clearly, less clutter," said Patrick.

"You are referring to what I call the deafening noise of opinions from your parents, teachers, and managers about what you should do or what they think you excel at. It all fades away. You are no longer aware of yourself. You are in a state of Flow, as the Positive Psychologist Mihaly Csikszentmihalyi puts it."

"This is so cool. I feel free in a way. It is clear what really matters to me," said Patrick.

"And what is that?" asked Reynold.

"What matters is learning and having challenges, to test the limits of what I can do and have fun. It is not about saving my job or making the organisation more successful. I could find another job elsewhere and the company could thrive without me," said Patrick.

After a few seconds of silence, he continued, "I need to organise a seminar and bring the team here so they find out about what they love."

"Thankfully, there are cheaper ways to do this," said Reynold.

"I am all ears," said Patrick.

"Spot on, Patrick. Planet Listening is our next stop," said Reynold, smiling.

They both said their goodbyes to Colin and left the building, back to the train, and then the ship.

## QUESTIONS

What were you doing the last time you lost track of time?

What type of task comes easy for you in your professional environment?

How much do you know about where your teammates find love in their work activities?

## ADVICE & EXPERIMENTATION

Encourage team members to dedicate part of their workweek to projects they're passionate about, aligning with the company's goals. Google has what they called the "20% time" policy, where they advise employees to engage in initiatives that interest them and might benefit the company.

5.3

# PLANET LISTENING

After a brief trip, they landed on Planet Listening. Its landscape was acoustically alive, with natural amphitheatres and echoing valleys that carried and amplified sounds gently across distances. Its atmosphere contained a heavier gas which facilitated the propagation of vibrations. If they were lucky, they would find Whispering Caverns.

Patrick and Reynold, in the middle of nowhere, walked on a pathway. They met a teenage boy called Billy.

"Hello, do you know where the closest town is?" asked Reynold.

"It is a few miles from here. You need to follow the 'Clinton' signs along the way," said Billy.

"Like the former U.S. President on Earth?" asked Patrick.

"Yes, he is a regular visitor. He is known for being a skilled listener," said Billy.

"I had no idea!"

"There is another town called Disraeli, named after another politician."

"Is it a British politician?"

"Yes, in the 19th century. There is a legend about the 1874 Prime Minister election."

"What legend?" asked Patrick.

"There was a woman who had the opportunity to have dinner with each competitor a week before the ballot. One was Mr Gladstone, a man of power, solar, ample gesture and imposing posture. On the other end, there was Mr Disraeli, a weighted man, luminous, discreet gestures, and measured posture. You could imagine the journalists waiting for hours at the restaurant door to get some insights and fresh information to influence the polls. They asked the woman as soon as she got out. 'Madam, madam, please, how was your dinner with Mr Gladstone?'. And the woman replied, 'I had a wonderful evening. I am under the impression that Mr Gladstone is the most intelligent person in the UK'. The following evening at another restaurant with as many journalists as the day before. Same question from the journalist, 'Madam, madam, please, how was your dinner with Mr Disraeli?'. And she replied, 'I had a wonderful evening. I am under the impression of being the most intelligent person in the UK'. Who do you think won the election?"

"It sounds like Disraeli won, even if it would make more sense for Gladstone, the person with supposedly the greatest intellect to be leading the country, wouldn't it?" said Patrick.

"Also, if I am not mistaken, Gladstone preceded and succeeded Disraeli as Prime Minister," said Reynold.

"You are both correct, but the point of the story is Disraeli was a skilled listener and known for being interested in those he interacted with. When you listen to people, they would follow your lead, as they are happy with their own behaviour and find themself pretty interesting around you," said Billy.

"You're a smart boy," said Reynold.

Patrick and Reynold continued walking on the path until they arrived in a small town with a 'Listening' tower. A structure that would capture and relay sounds from the environment. They could hear a classical music concert coming from the main natural amphitheatre. They joined the crowd and enjoyed the quartet.

During the break, they met with Nancy.

"How's the concert going so far for you?" asked Patrick.

"It is not my favourite type of music, but it helps me recharge my batteries," said Nancy.

"Why is that?"

"It takes a lot of energy to listen to my team. And some have a lot to say."

"I completely get it. I am a manager too. It makes me think of Jo, one of my employees. He just can't stop talking. He would always come to my office while I am busy."

"They all do."

"That's right. But when it's Jo, I would just pretend to pay attention while working on my computer. Sometimes, I would gaze at him, even smile. But he does not get it. I always end up telling him what to do, to make this torrent of words stop."

"I bet you are both frustrated at the end of the conversation. You are worried because of the time you have been wasting on your work and Jo is feeling unheard," said Nancy.

Patrick was silent, thinking about what she just said. Then Nancy continued, "I used to do this too, trying to get my teammates to leave me alone. But I realised it takes as much energy to fight it, rather than listening to them."

"What do you do to listen to your team?"

"There are a lot of ways to listen. What helped me was to let go. I am always busy, but I try to assess how critical is the work I am doing compared to supporting a teammate. If I am under a lot of pressure with a tight deadline, I will make sure not to be disturbed and let my team know I won't be available during that period of time. But if the task at hand can wait for a bit, then I would make myself available. I would turn off my computer screens to have a proper conversation."

"Reynold," said Patrick, "I need to return to Earth. Things must change."

They both greeted Nancy, wished her a nice concert and made their way back to the spacecraft.

## QUESTIONS

Remind yourself the last time when you experienced being truly heard. What did the listener do to make you feel that way?

How often do you find yourself formulating responses while someone else is talking?

When you're eager to share your thoughts and waiting for the first opportunity to say it, what emotions or sensations do you experience? Where in your body do these feelings manifest?

## ADVICE & EXPERIMENTATION

Eye contact - There have been studies about the fact that visual connection stimulates the secretion of the Oxytocin. It is the hormone known for bonding. You build trust when you look in the eyes.

Stop cutting-off people - You are smart, they are aware of it. You don't need to show them you already get it. Let them find their own words to articulate whatever they want to express. Silence is also a great tool to allow others to think.

Be curious - keep the ideas to yourself (oh yeah, this is hard, I have a lot of them), enable people to reveal their full imagination. Only ask questions, inquire for more details, more definitions because sometimes it seems obvious what they mean by using a certain word, but you might not have the same definition.

5.4

# ANOTHER TIME OUT ON PLANET EARTH - MILKY WAY

Patrick and Reynold listened to the broadcast of the second half of the concert on their journey back home. Once they landed, Patrick went back to his office and Reynold to a Toastmasters event to practise public speaking for his next conference.

Within a few days of returning to work, the same situation with Jo coming to Patrick's desk for a chat took place.

"Hey boss, is it a good time? I have something I'd like to run by you," said Jo.

"Sure, please just give a minute so I can finish this email," said Patrick. He finished it and put his computer to sleep. With unwavering focus, he locked his gaze on Jo, every cell in his body attuned and listening. He had not quite reached the level of Deepak Chopra, who teaches how to listen through the heart and the soul. Regardless, his teammate noticed something had changed this time.

"Alright, tell me," said Patrick with a smile.

"We will be in trouble with 'you know who' if we continue to work this way around their budget," said Jo. 'You know who' was a customer he always complained about.

"What do you mean?" asked Patrick, showing interest.

"Well, they are buying two days of our service per month. But 30% of it is being lost inefficiently. If we were to do all the jobs in one go, it would cost them less overall, and it won't affect other projects. This is not how we work. I understand the constraints of the business and that the money aspect is important, but we won't make this customer happy. They are paying too much for the value we offer."

"I see. You make a good point. We want our customers to be satisfied, and your team to be efficient, so what do you suggest we do?"

"I think we need to catch up with them. We explain the situation and recommend going into project mode. They should understand this is the way we deliver projects and that we can provide great value."

"OK, it sounds reasonable. Do you mind preparing an estimate to complete this work ahead of the meeting?" asked Patrick.

"Yes, of course. I'll get on it right away."

"Thanks."

Patrick called Reynold on the phone to tell him about what had just happened.

"Well done, Patrick, how do you feel?" said Reynold.

"I am proud of myself. I believe Jo is content too. He has vented less than usual. It did not take as much time and cherry on the cake, we agreed on a solution! I understand it might not always happen, but it is promising."

"I can see you've also applied the circular causality principle of the Systemic Approach. You changed the message. You got a different response," said Reynold and then continued, "What would you like to do now? Exploring another galaxy?"

"Maybe another time? I learnt a lot, and things start to get moving here. I am good for now," said Patrick with a faint smile on his face.

They hung up and agreed to meet again later in the year.

# 6

# AND THEY LIVED HAPPILY EVER AFTER... OR NOT

About 6 months after Patrick met with Reynold and started to explore the universe of Management, they went to a nice coffee shop, but without hot sauces this time.

"First," said Reynold, "I wanted to congratulate you, Patrick, for all the efforts you have made and for getting out of your comfort zone so many times. This is inspiring."

"Thank you. This is definitely difficult. It seems inevitable to pay a certain price, and to experience discomfort, to get results."

"Indeed, so tell me, what has happened with your team since we met?"

"I've been journaling. It helped me understand quite a few things about myself. In some situations, I adapted my behaviour instead of having my standard reaction and regretting it later."

"OK, great, what else?"

"The atmosphere at the office is a lot better. I am not afraid of getting the old complaints anymore. I am not sure if it is because they feel heard, or because of the greater sense of ownership over their job, but they are more satisfied and joyful. Don't get me wrong, they are not best friends, and I am not theirs either, but our relationship is more harmonious."

"It might be both indeed. What else did you notice?"

"I should have started with this, but we reached the goals and saved our division! I am the most surprised by these results."

"Congrats! How come you are surprised?"

"Well, I did not see how we could turn around the situation from where I sat. But this exploration, with trial and error, changed my perspective completely. As I mentioned, the team is a lot more engaged, resulting in a 20% increase in their billable. They also require little input from me since they are looking after the 'How'. Of course, I am still involved when they come to me for support on some important matters, but overall, we can say they became more autonomous."

"What are the benefits that you've noticed from your team becoming more independent?"

"I have a lot more time to focus on strategy and sales, which helped in turning the situation around. It is counterintuitive, but I found out that some services we provided, even though they were generating profits, had a tremendous impact on the performance of the team. It was disturbing them and affected their work on higher margin projects. So, I cut those off, which was a difficult discussion with my management."

"And you mentioned you had more time to focus on sales."

"Yes, I am proud to have closed one of the biggest deals of the company."

"Wow, congrats!"

"Thanks, and thank you, Reynold, for supporting me on this journey," said Patrick.

"I am glad I could help. What's next?" said Reynold.

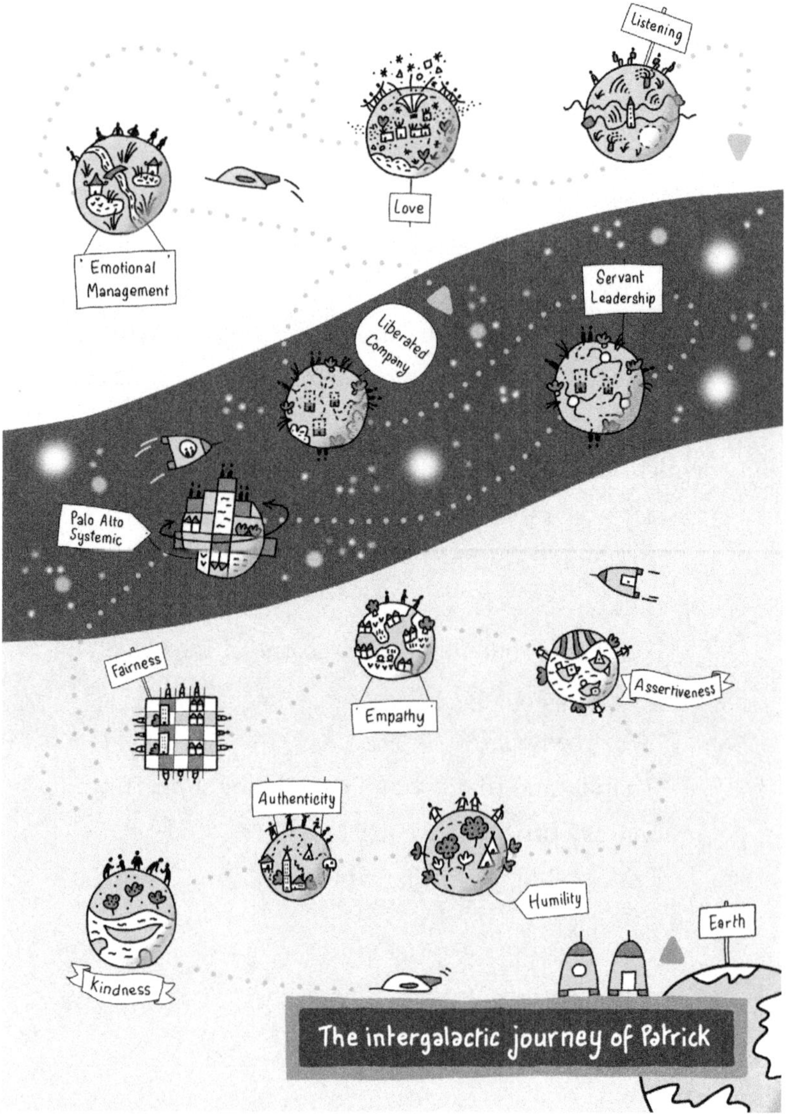
Listening
Love
Emotional Management
Servant Leadership
Liberated Company
Palo Alto Systemic
Fairness
Empathy
Assertiveness
Authenticity
Humility
Kindness
Earth
The intergalactic journey of Patrick

# *WHAT'S NEXT?*

Interesting question, what's next? Is there an end to this exploration? This universe of management is forever expanding, so we know we can't explore it all, but should we keep trying? Is it possible to reach a point where no further discovery is required for a manager? Would that be a need or a want? Hmmm.

If you look at Patrick's example, we have seen his itinerary. It does not mean that someone else would learn the same lessons if they were to take the same route. Also, there is a possibility that by taking an alternate path, they would get the same positive results.

The Anti-Hero Coach would say that people evolve, grow and the situation changes. All those factors are always moving, living. So, keeping on exploring, at a different pace and time, would be very beneficial.

Please don't be one of those frogs from "Five Frogs on a Log: A CEO's Field Guide to Accelerating the Transition in Mergers, Acquisitions, and Gut Wrenching Change" by Mark L. Feldman and Michael F. Spratt. Their story is the following: Five frogs are sitting on a log. Four decide to jump off. How many frogs remain? Answer: five. Why? Because there's a difference between deciding and doing.

One thing I would love you to take away from this book is to get into action mode.

What is the small step you could undertake to continue/start your exploration?

Please share your journey with me on LinkedIn: https://www.linkedin.com/in/renaudvandewalle/

## AUTHOR DISCLAIMER ALERT

Of course, the definition and interpretation of all those galaxies and planets are arguable, and I am convinced there are ways to fully embrace each of them. I just wanted to highlight the confusion and complexities that managers can interpret when introduced to these principles or qualities they might want to develop.

What is certain is you cannot force it. One needs to have a willingness to explore a planet to take full benefit.

Patrick has been brave to volunteer and explore all those planets. However, not all of them are for everyone, and that's OK. How boring would this be back on our beautiful Earth, if we all visited the same planets, took the same itinerary and if we were having all the same experiences? That would be scary, don't you think?

# ABOUT THE AUTHOR

'Anti-Hero Management' is inspired by my professional journey, offering insights into a mindset shift I discovered and refined over the years, providing readers with a way of thinking which facilitates developing their unique styles. Since 2010, I have led multicultural teams across Australia, Indonesia, Canada, and the UK, fuelled by my passion for human relations.

My career started as a developer for the first 6 months, straight after my IT Engineering Masters Degree, and I quickly moved into management roles. In 2018, I revitalised a struggling London-based company, marking a pivotal moment in my professional life by shifting my managerial approach. I held the position of Operations Director in that firm for a few years before being offered the opportunity to become the CEO. This presented an enormous challenge for me. I found myself in a situation where I felt I had nothing to lose, as, if I continued as I was doing in my previous role, it would fail. It was difficult, but I consider myself lucky to have faced this difficulty. It forced me to get out of my comfort zone and to question my way of managing. As a result, the team became more autonomous, I enjoyed working with them, the KPIs improved and within a year, the results were very positive. After this experience, I decided it was time for me to assist other managers, who may never encounter what I did, to make it happen and enable them to take a significant leap in their own exploration.

By 2023, after earning my ICF coaching certification, I founded Anti-Hero Management, advocating for personalized leadership to drive broader societal impact. To learn more about how Anti-Hero Management is supporting its clients on their management journey, visit:

https://antiheromanagement.com/

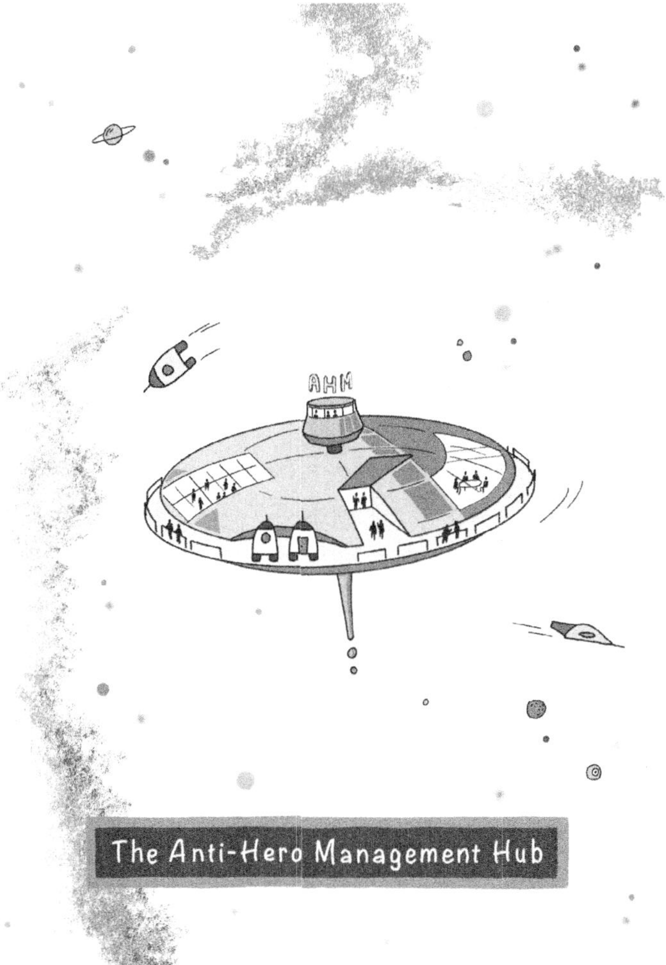
AHM
The Anti-Hero Management Hub

# THANK YOU NOTE

I would like to first thank you for reading this book. It means you have an interest in growing and you already took a first step (or another one) which contributes to my mission.

I would like to thank my wife Karine Vandewalle (formerly Roujas), with whom we have been exploring life together since 2008, travelling the world, having beautiful kids (no bias whatsoever). This book and the company would not exist without her support for all those years. Thank you to my parents for their support, too.

Thank you to Loïc Blandel, my business partner and long-time friend, for joining me on that entrepreneurial journey and for having actively taken part in shaping the Anti-Hero Management mindset.

To all the key people who trusted me over the years and for being their apprentice - my former bosses, investors, teachers, suppliers & clients (in chronological order): Ashul Shah, Nicolas Meyer, Graham Hill, Oscar Macia, Steve Brain, Sam Tilley, John Mayhew, Katherine Kostereva, Anne Vandezande, Yves Vandezande, Catherine Benamoussa, Yves Marc, Anne Issermann.

To my (very) exclusive book club members: Renaud Feidt and Boris Pivaudran. As well as the beta-readers: Ivy Clark and Déodat Richard. The proof-reader: Kerry Mayes, and my publishing coach: Nathalie Bagadey. They made this book better, smoother, and possible.

To the entrepreneurs and authors who inspired me over the years: Mark Manson, Tom Bilyeu, Simon Sinek, Steven Bartlett, Alex Hormozi, Dan Sullivan, Tim Ferris, Codie Sanchez, Daniel Priestley, Nancy Kline, Marshall Goldsmith, Dale Carnegie, Rich Litvin, Steven Chandler.

# NOTES


PLANET KINDNESS

"Social Exchange Theory" developed by sociologist George C. Homans
https://en.wikipedia.org/wiki/Social_exchange_theory

"Ben Franklin effect"
https://en.wikipedia.org/wiki/Ben_Franklin_effect

PLANET AUTHENTICITY

"The power of vulnerability" - a Ted talk by Brené Brown
https://www.youtube.com/watch?v=iCvmsMzlF7o

PLANET HUMILITY

"The Perceived Impact of Leaders' Humility on Team Effectiveness: an Empirical Study" by A. Rego, M. Cunha, A. Simpson
https://link.springer.com/article/10.1007/s10551-015-3008-3

PLANET ASSERTIVENESS

"Sex differences in assertive behavior: An empirical investigation." by Hollandsworth, J. G., & Wall, K. E. (1977)
https://psycnet.apa.org/doiLanding?doi=10.1037%2F0022-0167.24.3.217

"Managing the Double Bind: Women Directors' Participation Tactics in the Gendered Boardroom" by Tiffany Trzebiatowski, Courtney McCluney, Morela Hernandez Published Online: 18 May 2022.

https://doi.org/10.1287/orsc.2022.1599
"Follow My Lead: Assertive Cheap Talk and the Gender Gap" by Shanthi Manian , Ketki Sheth
Published Online: 17 Feb 2021.
https://doi.org/10.1287/mnsc.2020.3837
"The 5 Vocal Foundations of Great Communication" - video by Vinh Giang on UNSTOPPABLE
https://www.youtube.com/watch?v=CuaY4qe4V34
"How to be CONCISE when you speak!" – video by Vinh Giang on youtube.
https://www.youtube.com/shorts/kHRwnqJgc4U
« How to STOP Being Ignored & Stand Out From The Crowd! » – video by Vinh Giang on youtube.
https://www.youtube.com/watch?v=YIn4YMEGJco

PLANET EMPATHY
"Brené Brown on Empathy" by THE RSA Org
https://www.thersa.org/
https://www.youtube.com/watch?v=1Evwgu369Jw
"The Empathy Problem: Mistaking a Rare Talent for a Business Necessity" by Todd M. Johnson - Gallup article
https://www.gallup.com/workplace/258041/empathy-problem-mistaking-rare-talent-business-necessity.aspx

PLANET FAIRNESS
"Surrounded by idiots" by Thomas Erikson
"How Fair Is Your Workplace?" by Brian Kropp, Jessica Knight, and Jonah Shepp
https://hbr.org/2022/07/how-fair-is-your-workplace
"The Chimp Paradox - The Mind Management Programme for Confidence, Success and Happiness" By Professor Steve Peters - Published 5 January 2012
"5 Benefits of Journaling for Mental Health" by Jeremy Sutton, Ph.D., Scientifically reviewed by Saima Latif, Ph.D. - Published 14 May 2018
https://positivepsychology.com/benefits-of-journaling/

PLANET PALO ALTO SYSTEMIC
Medical Research Institute (MRI)
https://mri.org/
Gregory Bateson, an anthropologist and social scientist who collaborated with the MRI

https://en.wikipedia.org/wiki/Gregory_Bateson

PLANET SERVANT LEADERSHIP

"Servant leadership as antecedent of trust in organizations" by Sen Sendjaya, Andre Pekerti
https://www.emerald.com/insight/content/doi/10.1108/01437731011079673/full/html
"Trust and performance in business teams: a meta-analysis" by Amy M. Morrissette, Jennifer L. Kisamore
https://www.emerald.com/insight/content/doi/10.1108/TPM-02-2020-0012/full/html
"The influence of servant leadership, trust in leader and thriving on employee creativity" by Neeraj Kumar Jaiswal, Rajib Lochan Dhar
https://www.emerald.com/insight/content/doi/10.1108/LODJ-02-2015-0017/full/html

PLANET OF LIBERATED COMPANY

"Freedom, Inc." by Brian M. Carney and Isaac Getz
"Failing Forward: Turning Mistakes into Stepping Stones for Success." by John C. Maxwell

PLANET EMOTIONAL MANAGEMENT

"The chimp paradox - The Mind Management Programme for Confidence, Success and Happiness" by Prof Steve Peters

PLANET LOVE

"Career Fit and Burnout Among Academic Faculty" by Tait D. Shanafelt, MD; Colin P. West, MD, PhD; Jeff A. Sloan, PhD; May 25, 2009
https://jamanetwork.com/journals/jamainternalmedicine/fullarticle/415000

PLANET LISTENING

Article "Listening = Engaging" by Renaud Vandewalle
https://antiheromanagement.com/listening-engaging/
"Time To Think - Listening To Ignite The Human Mind" by Nancy Kline